Wilf's dad wanted a party. He put up some lights.

1

Wilma and Dad made a barbecue.

Wilf and Mum took the food
outside.

Everyone helped.

The dads lit the fire.

The fire went out.

The children were hungry.

The dads lit the fire again.

It began to rain.

The dads cooked burgers.

The children were fed up.

The burgers burned.

"Yuk!" said Chip.

Oh no!

The dads got wet.

"Hooray!" said the children.